NEXT
YEAR

Text copyright © 2017 by Ruth Vander Zee   Illustrations copyright © 2017 by Gary Kelley
Edited by Amy Novesky and Kate Riggs   Designed by Rita Marshall
Published in 2017 by Creative Editions   P.O. Box 227, Mankato, MN 56002 USA
Creative Editions is an imprint of The Creative Company   www.thecreativecompany.us

Library of Congress Cataloging-in-Publication Data
Names: Vander Zee, Ruth, author. / Kelley, Gary, illustrator.
Title: Next Year: hope in the dust / by Ruth Vander Zee; illustrated by Gary Kelley.
Summary: As Calvin grows from childhood to adulthood, he and his parents endure four years
of dust storms and drought following "Black Sunday" in 1935, and he becomes determined to
preserve the land rather than exploit it. Includes historical note.
Identifiers: LCCN 2016056322 / ISBN 978-1-56846-282-0
Subjects: CYAC: 1. Droughts—Fiction. 2. Dust Bowl Era, 1931–1939—Fiction.
3. Great Plains—History—Fiction. BISAC: 1. JUVENILE NONFICTION/History/United States/20th Century.
2. JUVENILE NONFICTION/People & Places/United States/General.
3. JUVENILE NONFICTION/History/United States/General.
Classification: LCC PZ7.V285116 Nex 2017 / DDC [E]—dc23
First Edition 2 4 6 8 9 7 5 3 1

CREATIVE ⟨Z⟩ EDITIONS

NEXT

HOPE IN THE DUST

YEAR

RUTH VANDER ZEE illustrated by GARY KELLEY

BLACK SUNDAY

April 14, 1935

I remember that morning. So different from all the other mornings:

    Cool.

        Clear.

            A run-to-my-cousin's-house-and-play-outside,

windless,

hopeful

day.

But in the late afternoon ...

a dust cloud covers the north-to-south, east-to-west sky.

Like midnight in the middle of the day, without
moon and stars.

Biting winds blow knives of
sand into my skin.
I can't see my hand in front
of my face, and I crawl the two miles
home 'cause I can't stand up to the wind.

When I open the door, my ma is standing
in the kitchen. Ankle-deep in sand.
I run to her and take the shovel she's hold-
ing out of her hand.

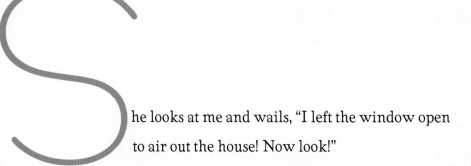

She looks at me and wails, "I left the window open to air out the house! Now look!"

Dad stares at the kerosene lamp flickering dull shadows on the wall. He looks like a beaten-up kid.

But he still sits there and says, just like he's been doing for the last four years, "It's gonna be better next year."

But I don't believe him.

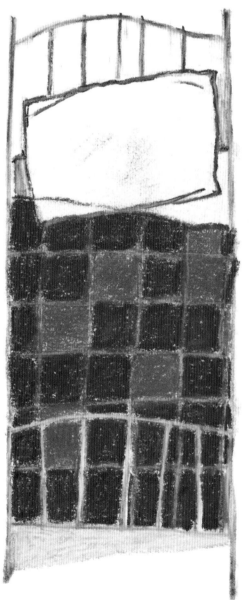

'm twelve years old, and right now, all I want is things to be like they were before the dust storms came:

Blue skies.

Rain.

Acres of golden wheat dipping and swaying in gentle breezes.

Enough money to add my very own bedroom onto our house.

I want my ma to smile and be pretty again without hard lines on her face.

I want

The milk in my glass to not look like it's sprinkled with pepper.

My whole pillowcase clean and white in the morning–not just the part where I put my head.

A bath on Saturday night with more than a cup of water.

To not cough all the time.

But what I have is
        Angry winds that take the topsoil and spit
it into the air.
Crops that wither before my eyes.
Our under-fed, scrawny cattle sold for a few cents a head.

Hungry rabbits invading by the thousands.
Grasshoppers eating the bark off the fence posts.
My classmates dying of dust pneumonia.
And four years of Dad saying,
"Next year it's gonna be better."

And it never is.

That night, Dad sees Ma standing ankle-deep in sand and cries.
I never saw my dad cry.

He looks at me and says, "Calvin, I had no idea. I brought
you and your ma out here because I knew I could make money
on this land ...

Me.

Somebody who never had anything all my growin' up."

"You did, Dad," I say. "You did real good for us. For a while."

"No, Calvin. I messed up. BAD.

I stopped plowing deep.

I skimmed all the buffalo grass away.

And then it stopped raining."

He sighs. "And what did we get? Four years of you and your ma eatin' this dust and dirt for breakfast, lunch, and dinner. That's not what a man does to his family."

After I see my dad so desperate, I know I have to pitch in.

I go to school, but any extra time I have, my teacher helps me research better ways to farm.

learn about contouring rows instead of plowing in straight lines.
About rotating crops instead of planting wheat year after year.
That helps. Some.

    For the next four awful, dust-blowing, never-getting-ahead years.

    For the next four years of families in our town leaving and
heading to the promised land of sunny California.

    But we stay.

    I have a knot in my stomach that never goes away.

    I never say anything, but it's there. Every day.

ut then ... towards the end of my sixteenth year,
a bluish cloud covers the north-to-south,
east-to-west sky.

It settles overhead.

Hopeful.

Promising.

A gentle rain falls.

The land takes a deep breath and sucks the water into itself.

And then, the thirsty ground takes great gulps from the
downpour that follows.

I run into the house, grab Ma's hand, and lead her outside.

She stands, looking up. "Is this it?" she whispers.

Dad comes over from the fields, sees Ma, and takes her in his arms.

That is the beginning of

The end of the drought.

The end of blowing dust every day.

The end of life as I knew it for nine years.

Because, after all those years of misery,

Dad says, "Calvin, your ma and I talked. We can't do this anymore."

"You're leaving now? After all we've been through?" I shout. "After all
these years of 'next year it's gonna be better'?"

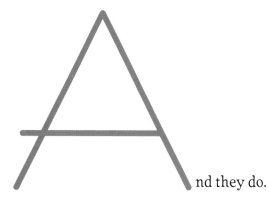

nd they do.

They pack up and take off.

I watch as the car fades into the distance.

I don't go with them.

Somehow, I can't leave.

In some strange way, I love what I've hated for so long.

I know it'll be hard, but I'm going to plow my father's fields on my own.

I look out at the small green shoots finally growing in our field and know that I am home.

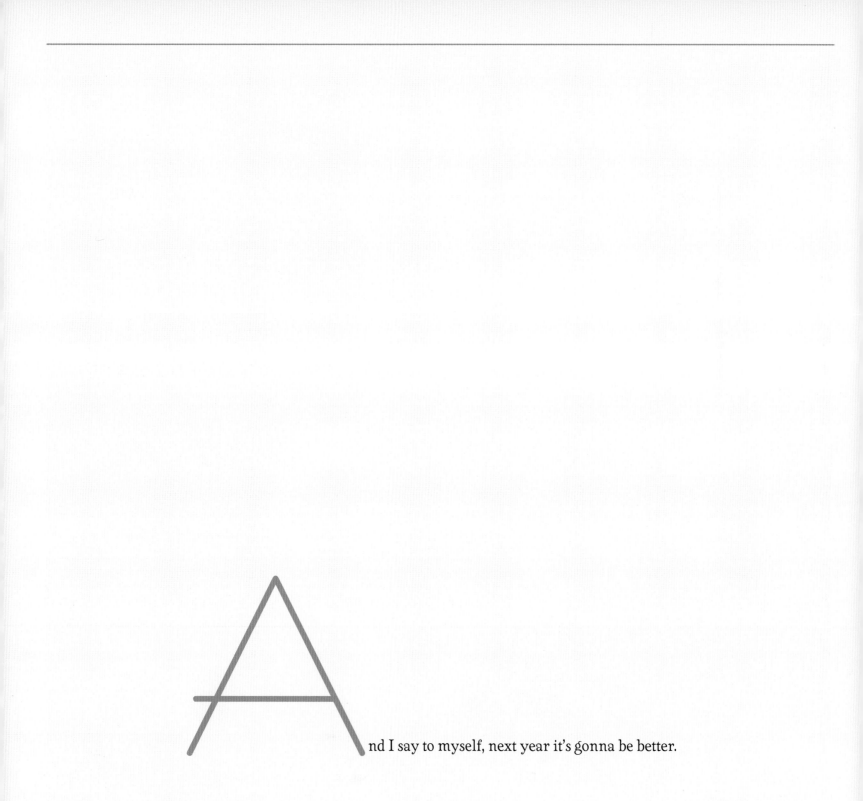

And I say to myself, next year it's gonna be better.

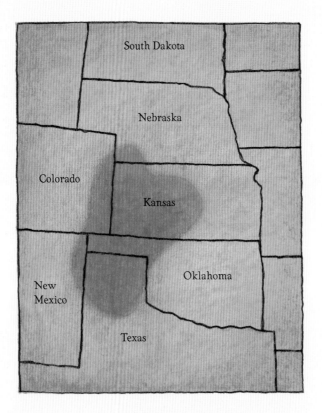

For those who lived in the Great Plains region known as the Dust Bowl between 1931 and 1939, a shared sense of hope that things were bound to get better was often the only thing that propelled them forward through the misery of everyday existence.

From the 1910s through the 1920s, the demand for wheat in America was great, and land was plentiful. Many people moved to the Great Plains to farm, turning native grasslands into millions of acres of fields. The weather was favorable, wheat prices were high, and the possibilities seemed endless. However, when rainfall decreased to about 10 inches per year in the early '30s and the winds started blowing, the dried-out topsoil became blizzards of dust as an 8-year drought set in. The incredible hardships of this time were made more terrible by the fact that the country as a whole was suffering through the Great Depression.

I became interested in this story when I heard that "next year" was a phrase voiced by so many during that time. Being raised near a farming community, I understood that sentiment. Those were people who persevered despite the difficulties that swirled all around them—obstacles that would have discouraged and defeated others.

I am humbled by their stories and their strength of character. — *R. V. Z.*